SHE SHOT

at The

MOON

SHE SHOT

at The

MOON

A Guided Journal

JANAE CHEYENNE

Charleston, SC
www.PalmettoPublishing.com

She Shot at the Moon

Copyright © 2020 by Janae Cheyenne

All rights reserved.

First Edition

Paperback ISBN: 978-1-64990-904-6
eBook ISBN: 978-1-64990-836-0

"SHOOT FOR THE MOON,
EVEN IF YOU FALL
YOU'LL LAND AMONGST THE STARS."

Dedicate to

Mrs. Trudgeon & My G-Baby:

*Thank you Mrs. Trudgeon for helping me to see my
talent of writing and pointing out my free spirit.
Look, I've actually started something and finished it!*

*GBaby, you told me that I needed to
write a book during the quarantine,
and I did it. I hope it makes you proud.*

BACKGROUND

As I look outside of my window, Mahogany Teakwood High Intensity candle unlit, eating a bag of Flamin' Hot White Cheddar popcorn, for a moment I've forgotten about the chaos going on in the world right now. I'm currently living in Kansas City, Missouri and we're on a COVID-19 lockdown until the end of April, but honestly who knows how long it will last. Hopefully by the time I finish writing this, I can say that life is back to normal. Not just any normal, but a new normal that is well overdue. I just moved to Missouri about a month prior and literally in a matter of days, life has turned upside down. My granny (GBaby is what we call her) keeps telling me I should write a book during this time. I've always wanted to write a book because honestly, the last few years of my life have been wild. And it continues to be that. So, her telling me to write the book, along, with the quarantine lockdown, gave me the fuel I needed to get it started.

Writing has always been an outlet for me. It's kind of second nature and something I enjoy doing. I would always keep a journal growing up, even if I didn't finish it. It's something special about documenting my personal interests and thoughts. I love it because I get to reflect and see my growth, even though I've realized I'm the same person I've always been, just older and a little more mature. I'm not sure what that exactly says about me. Anyways, I'm the youngest in my family. One sister, she's one of my favorite people in the world, and three older brothers (one passed at birth and two half brothers). My sister and I are eight years apart, so I think that gap may have led me to doing a lot of things on my own. Reading and writing were always two hobbies of mine. Have you ever seen someone go to the mall and only want to sit in Barnes & Noble all day? That was young Janae. My sister hated it. Aside from that, my writing catalogue mainly consisted of songs and poems. My hit song, entitled Candy Girl, was inspired by Diamond from the Crime Mob's verse of Rock Ya Hips. My prize-winning poem, Poor Man, received the lamination award from my granddaddy. So basically, I deserve a Pulitzer Prize or something.

As you can see, writing has always been a part of me. As I get older, it's more therapeutic than anything. Over the past years, my life has been a whirlwind of constant transitions, adaptations, lessons, and ultimately growth. Through it all, writing has helped me to study myself, get over heartbreaks, manifest my goals, and refresh myself spiritually. For the first time, I completed not one but *two* journals, cover to cover. I am now working on my third one and baby, trust me, when I tell you there's a lot of life and discovery in these journals. I'm so happy to have documented every emotion. There's been success, uncertainty, confusion, and anything else you can imagine. I hope that you can read through my experiences and follow the journal prompts I have given to help you navigate whatever you're going through. Or, maybe you just simply need something to entertain you. That's fine too! Enjoy!

> *"Written from the heart, a book is the best way*
> *to show you who I am. And make an impact."*
>
> —Laila Ali

#1 JOURNAL PROMPT

Current Life Status

When starting a new journal, I like to begin with a "Current Life Update" page. On this page, I include my current life status, any hobbies & interests I have at the time, my current job or school status, relationship status, etc. Anything that you feel is important to you in this current moment will be great to write on this page. As you go through your journal, continue to look at this page and see how many things change or what stays the same. Either way, it's great to have something to reflect on and see either your staying power or progress.

At the end, include your current goals. Make sure that you are specific with your goals and give yourself deadlines to look toward.

AGE: _____

CURRENT LOCATION: _____

CURRENT OCCUPATION: _____

CURRENT HOBBIES/INTERESTS: _____

_____

RELATIONSHIP STATUS: _____

WHAT'S ON YOUR MIND: _____

_____

CURRENT GOALS: _____

_____

_____

_____

_____

_____

_____

_____

_____

PART ONE

Decision To Go To Tuskegee

To start my story, I am going to take you back to the day I fell in love with the illustrious and historic Tuskegee University. Here is where my adult journey began. Without me going to Tuskegee, I wouldn't be the woman I am now.

It started with a trip to Alabama State University for their open house. I went along with my mother, sister, and best friend. I knew from the start I didn't want to go there, and we just toured the campus without paying the actual school any mind. On the way home, one of my sister's best friends asked us to stop at Tuskegee, which we would pass through on the way back to Atlanta. I remembered going there in the 9th grade, but college wasn't even a thought in my mind at that time. So, we went to Tuskegee and the moment I stepped out of the car, it was like the ancestors spoke to me. Honestly, I'm not sure if it was the way the sun hit the well-manicured grass or if the heat just brainwashed me or something, but I felt connected to that little place. My sister's friend told me that their open house was coming up and it happened to be the same weekend of Savannah State University's open house. I loved Savannah State and me and my best friend, Tae, planned on going there together. We had already been down there for a basketball game and knew people there, so we weren't unfamiliar with campus life. All in all, I decided to go to Tuskegee's open house just to see what was so special about that school.

A few weeks later, my mom and I packed up the car and went to good ole Tuskegee, Alabama for a second time. Now, if you've never been to Tuskegee, then let me explain it to you. You head down 85 South and go from Atlanta's city traffic to clear skies and "trees, trees, and more trees" as a classmate described in an assignment (they got a passing grade on that too!).

Tuskegee is a gem. We don't have a Walmart and the best restaurant there at the time would be a toss-up between the Coop and Cornbread Fred's, which have both since sadly closed down. But at the same time, we have a hotel on campus and not one, but three historical landmarks on our campus. I love everything about Tuskegee. When I went down there for the open house, I had no clue how strong that love would grow to be.

I'm not the most social person, so arriving on campus and entering the gym for open house was EXTRA. I was not enthused by all of the school ambassadors in my face screaming "T-U" and club officials running up to me. I probably had a mean resting face as I made my way to the cheerleading table to see my God sister. She was the only other person I knew at Tuskegee, so it only made sense that I stopped there. We chopped it up for a bit and then up into the stands I went for the show.

Open house is a true production. The cheerleaders, the Greeks, and even the current students pump so much life into you, as the band plays the infamous, Ball N- Parlay. Literally, the entire arena is standing up and vibing singing "Whether sunny or grey, we gon' ball and parlay, we get drunk everyday, that's the Tuskegee way". As you're swaying back and forth, you're trying to understand these words that they're singing so passionately. You're wondering, "how can I learn these words and be as happy as they are?" Before you can even finish sitting down, someone blurts over the microphone, "pay your deposit now, only $500 right now!" and your mom looks at you and it's time to make the biggest decision of your life.

Of course, I said yes!

I wanted to ball and parlay, get drunk every day, and learn the Tuskegee way. And that my friends is how I chose Tuskegee. But there's a little saying that you don't choose Tuskegee, Tuskegee chooses you!

FRESHMAN YEAR/FIRST REAL LOVE

My first week at Tuskegee didn't quite go as well as I would've liked, but I will never forget it. It was just us freshmen there for orientation week. There were parties every night. For the most part, I spent time with my sister's friend. Eventually I started mingling with a few other people I had met around campus or over Freshman Group Chats. There was a block party on the basketball court near Younge Hall and in the midst of party- ing, my auntie called me with the most traumatic and unexpected news I've ever heard.

One of my childhood friends went for a tackle during their exhibition football game and passed away on the field. Shaking, I called someone for confirmation and almost instantly my legs gave out and I hit the ground. One thing about me, I never cry in front of people, but I couldn't even help it this time. I'm thankful for the people who helped me that night, people who grew to become my friends after that night.

I knew I couldn't go back to my dorm just yet, so I drowned myself in Paul Masson and tried to mask how I felt. Unfortunately, that night I cried until my eyes looked as if I had just lost a boxing match. My cousin saw a couple of my tweets about me not being able to sleep and showed my mom.

The next morning my mom was there to bring me home for the candlelight vigil. This was the first death that really hit me and the fact that I would've been at that game had I not been in Tuskegee, was a thought that kept playing over in my mind. Growing up in the church, I was pretty spiritual but I had never gotten on my knees to pray. Since the tears wouldn't stop, I decided this would be my first, but it surely wouldn't be my last. My personal spiritual journey began the day I prayed in my room, asking God to stop my eyes from crying. I knew that I would have to go back to school in a few days and nothing but God's strength could help me get through it.

After a couple of days at home, I went back down to Tuskegee to officially start classes. Quickly, I met my college best friends in the most random ways and we explored that city for everything it was worth. Whether we were standing on our bench in the Soul Inn (one of our only clubs) dying from the smoke or just chilling on the gazebo, watching everybody on The Yard, we found something to do. There's so much I don't remember, due to being under the influence about 75% of the time but what I do remember is gold. Tuskegee teaches you so much from how to survive with nothing but the art of finesse. Also, if you didn't have a crazy love story, you were a lucky one. Sadly, I dealt with one and honestly, it could have all been avoided, but things happen how they should and I won't question God. Plus, it left a great story to tell.

My roommate Morgan and I should have known things weren't going to go well the moment our other roommate left to go out with one of our friends. The two of them together were trouble. You see, when it came to the four of us, I would be the most responsible and that's pretty scary. So, you can only imagine what's about to happen. I couldn't go out because I was being a great girlfriend and chose to spend time with my boyfriend. We can call him Cain. Morgan stayed home with a headache. I remember getting a text around 11 or so saying that our friends couldn't find each other at the bar. All I could do was shake my head and hope they made it home safe. Hours later, there was a knock at my room door and somebody sounding like a child calling for their mom. "Janaeeeee! Janaeeeee!" Now imagine that slurred, dragged, and coming from somebody in tears. I open the door and there's Chi, my other roommate and Mya, a mutual friend of ours.

Mya is out of it, walks into the room and plops on the couch. Chi was on the floor, just yelling my name. So Morgan and I wrestle with her, trying to get her in the bed, but she kept doing the dumbest stuff like saying "You can't box me in like a zoo animal!" While that madness was going on, Mya was passed out on the couch, throwing up. I'm pretty sure she was supposed to be poisoned that night because we sprayed Lysol all over her face trying to clean up the couch.

I occasionally went to check on my boyfriend, but in hindsight, I could've done more than just leaving him in the room. Then things took a major turn. A friend of Chi's came over and of course, he was drunk too! We were talking in the kitchen when he fell, out of a bar chair, in slow motion.

I already didn't care for this guy being with Chi and his sloppiness didn't help. After getting up, me and him went outside to talk about Chi when all hell broke loose. As I was explaining my disapproval of Chi and the guy's situationship, Morgan came outside to warn me that Cain was pissed and on the way. The moment Cain came outside, he misinterpreted the situation, not understanding why his girlfriend was outside alone with another guy in the middle of the night. When the drunken guy decided to defuse the situation by explaining how me and him were "friends", it only made it worse. Tempers began to flare. The girls and I tried our best to break up the fight. Eventually Chi left with the drunken guy and Cain stormed out, while I was left trying to process what had just happened.

It was just a drunk, confusing night full of misunderstanding. Unfortunately, our relationship was never the same after that. After a couple of years of not speaking and avoiding each other, we actually can have a genuine convo and I'm thankful for that. The craziest thing is following the day that we finally talked after this incident, two things happened. First, I got a call offering me an internship in Kansas City and then my granddaddy passed away from cancer.

JOURNAL PROMPT #2

New Beginnings, Lessons Learned From Experiences

One important thing I like to do in my journal is document new beginnings, such as the start of each new school year. I like to share my expectations, express my feelings, and set goals. Also, when I am faced with issues like the one with my boyfriend, I like to take the time to see what I could have done differently in the situation. With anything, I try to learn all I can from it.

What are your expectations and feelings of this new journey in your life? List your specific goals for this area of your life.

_____

_____

_____

_____

_____

_____

_____

_____

_____

_____

_____

_____

_____

_____

PART TWO

Losing Granddaddy

My mom arrived in Tuskegee to pick me up for summer break and the moment she walked into my apartment, I knew something was up. My mom told me that my granddaddy lost his battle with cancer. He had been fighting it for the past few years and was recently back in the hospital. The cancer slowly took him away from us. With me away at college, I missed watching his body change and sadly, I'm happy for that. Most of the last memories with my granddaddy were how I always remembered him and not the person that cancer left after abusing his body. My granddaddy was the protector of our family. A purple heart Army veteran who wouldn't say a word until you got him started on something political. At that point, you couldn't get him to stop. My favorite memories with him will always be our car rides, picking me up from school. I would hop in the car and nine times out of ten I would sit on his gun and have to hand it over. He would always bring me a bag of chips & lemonade wrapped in aluminum foil, to keep it cold. Riding down 166, no more than 25 mph with a trail of cars behind us and me faking sleep so I didn't have to listen to his rants about how crazy the world was. If only he knew how much crazier it could get. Then if my granny hadn't cooked, he'd take me to Mrs. Winners on Campbellton Rd. and remind me to get a gallon of sweet tea, flashing a smile that showed his gold tooth. No matter how embarrassed I would be by his slow driving or when he would roll down the window to tell the kids at school to "pull up your pants and get out the street," I cherished those car rides. That's all I could think of during the car ride back to Atlanta with my mom. A few tears rolled down my face, but it kind of scared me that I didn't react like I would have expected myself to. That's something I've learned: grief hits you when you least expect it sometimes. It may be years but it'll happen one day.

A week after being home, we celebrated the life of my granddaddy and a couple of weeks after that I was packed up and on my way to Kansas City, Missouri for my first internship. I honestly expected this to just be a quick learning experience for the summer. Little did I know, this would be the first introduction to my new home for the next three years.

KC INTERNSHIP

How does a little Georgia Peach who never lived outside of Southwest Atlanta end up in Kansas City, Missouri? I'll tell you!

My older cousin lived there, and an internship opened at a professional sports team in the area. I wanted to work in sports and entertainment, so I applied.

Did I expect to even get the internship? Not at all. Surprised wasn't even the word when they called to offer me the internship. After getting off the phone with the recruiter, I called my cousin to ask if I could stay at his place since he wouldn't be there over the summer. He said yes and that sealed the deal!

When I tell you, I lived the life that summer. Living rent free in an apartment in one of the best areas of the city, driving my mom's car, and making pretty good money for a fresh 20-year-old. I took on the role as the Food & Beverage Intern at Kauffman Stadium, the home of the Kansas City

Royals. I never worked at a baseball stadium before, so I had no clue what to expect. I talked with the HR manager and shared my interest in learning everything there was to learn about the business. We created a rotation that allowed me to work in every department from culinary to retail. I spent a few weeks with each department and a little extra in those that I had the most interest in, like the Premium department. My major at Tuskegee was Hospitality Management and I've always known that I wanted to work with events. Working in the Premium department, I was able to work two of the major events for the Royals, Big Slick's Charity Gala and the Royals Diamond of Dreams Fundraising Event. Those were the first major events that I ever worked, and I knew that I didn't want them to be my last. The two fundraisers solidified my love for events and that summer immersed me in the world of sports and entertainment that I love. While work kept me extremely busy, sometimes working 12-14 hour days and up to eight consecutive days, I was still able to do a little self-discovery during my off time.

JOURNAL PROMPT #3

Monthly Recaps

With this internship being such a new experience for me, I knew that I had to do more than just work day after day. I have always had the mindset that every work experience is nothing more than a learning experience. I am a person that learns by working hands on and then taking detailed notes. Since everything was so new, I decided to record notes, recapping each department rotation. I knew this would be beneficial somewhere along the line. I continued to do this even after my internship ended and I just changed it to be a monthly life recap. I started to include any major events that happened during the month, even things outside of work. I usually go through the pictures in my phone to refresh my memory, so that I don't miss anything. My monthly recaps are now one of the staples in all of my journals!

Share all of your highlights and low points of the month. What have you learned? How did these events make you feel? What goals do you have for the upcoming month?

_____

_____

_____

_____

_____

_____

_____

_____

_____

_____

_____

_____

_____

BREAK UP/LIVING ALONE

When I first moved up to KC for my internship, my family thought it would be a great idea for my granny to live with me for the first few weeks since she was still dealing with my granddaddy's passing. It was my first time living away from home, by myself in a new city. It really was great for her because I know she needed a getaway and it did help me to get adjusted. But once she moved back to Atlanta and I really had this condo to myself, I was really in my element. I have always been a loner in a sense, and I love to be by myself. Something about living in your own space, moving how you want, when you want just gives me life. So many people would ask if I got bored or anything, but trust me, I spent so much time at work with thousands of people, that whenever I was at home, I literally didn't want to see another soul. I never really had time to go out, so I didn't mind the fact that I didn't have any friends there. I might have gone out two or three times my entire summer there.

Also when I first moved to KC, me and Cain were back and forth. After a few weeks I realized that a relationship was just not for me at the time. I was coming into my own and I knew that our relationship was one that could last forever if we wanted, but I knew I wasn't ready to commit to that. That is something I pride myself on. I will put myself and my true feelings first, even if it may hurt the other person at the time. In my opinion, it's better than being further along the road and then wondering "is there more?" or "am I missing out on something?", which is totally normal for someone in their 20s. You have to be completely honest with yourself. So, with that relationship completely ending, I really didn't talk to anyone seriously for that entire summer. It was just me and work. I began getting more in tune with my spiritual side and diving into myself a little more. I was figuring out just what I wanted to do in life, since I would only have one semester left after this summer. That might have been one of the best summers for me. It's funny because so often I hear people say how Summer 16 was so lit and fun, but mine was like an underground grind. One that set me up for everything that was to come.

JOURNAL PROMPT #4

Letter to Myself/Past or Future

This may be one of the most common journal prompts, but that is because it is so important when it comes to reflection and growth.

Write a letter to yourself, past or future. Share where you currently are in life and give yourself advice.

_____

_____

_____

_____

_____

_____

_____

_____

_____

_____

_____

_____

_____

_____

PART THREE

Last Semester of School/ Struggle Living #1

I only had about 2 weeks to get things together after coming home from Kansas City. I spent that time with family, then packed up to complete my Tuskegee experience. I only had one semester left and wasn't quite sure what I would do next. I knew I had a few options, but there wasn't anything final. Time was ticking. Honestly, I should have known that this semester would be a wild ride the moment we touched down. Since I would only be in Tuskegee for a semester, I decided to just crash on the couch of my friends' apartment. We decided I could just put in on the rent and things would be perfect. It was my roommates from the year before, so we already knew what to expect living with each other. However, our expectations for this new apartment were too high. I mean, wayyyy too high.

We arrived at the University Terrace anticipating a lavish, new, off-campus apartment. It was going to be furnished, have wifi and cable, all new appliances, and most importantly was going to be newly renovated.

Well, let's see. When we walked in, we had roaches and a roof. Oh, and a fridge. I would say an oven, but our gas wasn't turned on yet. Which meant, we couldn't really cook. Our tub was still under construction, so we couldn't take showers. We had to search the other apartments to pull together the furniture that was promised. It took weeks for our cable to get turned on, so we rotated ATL and The Notebook on DVD every night. I'm sure I'm missing stuff, but you get the picture. It was real life insane. The company promised housing to more people than they could physically hold. Some people didn't even have a building to live in, so I guess we should've been thankful.

But honestly, we were thankful for our friends at Tuskegee. We would have a 3-for-1 package where we would go to our friend's house and they would let us take showers at their place. Their gift in return would be a meal, but it helped us out too since we didn't have any gas for our stove yet. After around two months, we finally got a completed apartment. When I tell you, that was a humbling experience. Every living experience in Tuskegee is humbling actually. If you can make it out of Tuskegee, you can make it anywhere in my opinion. Although we had our struggles, it's still one of the most beautiful places I've ever known. I love that school and everything about it. It's a feeling you'll only understand once you've stepped on the campus of Mother Tuskegee.

JOURNAL PROMPT #5

Sermon, Self Help, Lecture, Book Notes

It's important to fill your mind with positive and motivational words, especially when your environment isn't ideal. Reading books, listening to podcasts, and watching sermons are lectures are great ways to get yourself in the right mindset.

Pick a motivational video, podcast, or book and take detailed notes in your journal.

_____

_____

_____

_____

_____

_____

_____

_____

_____

_____

_____

_____

_____

_____

NEW RELATIONSHIP

As I was closing my chapter at Tuskegee, a brand new chapter of my life was forming. This chapter was very unfamiliar and yet, amazing. This was the first time I fell head over heels in love. It was so unexpected and even now, I think of how a lot of heartbreak could have been avoided. However, I know that every second spent was crucial to creating the woman I am now. We can call him Ford. I knew him from playing football with my cousins. After a little IG flirting, we finally got on the phone. And that first night, we literally talked *all* night. I remember the movie ATL had to have played on repeat at least three times in the background. Our conversation never ended. From that conversation, even though we attended schools in different states, we were inseparable. We would wake up, get on Facetime and never get off the phone. It didn't matter if we were in class, in meetings, or out at parties. I know, so extra.

One weekend came up when Ford and my cousins had a football game. I went up with my mom and best friend. He ended up meeting my mom after the game and that was not my plan. Anybody who knows me, knows I don't introduce anyone to my family. I just don't like to have my family create any expectations when I don't even know where the relationship may end up. When it comes to relationships, I am extremely private. Nevertheless, they met and that was the first night I stayed with him. I remember leaving to go back to Tuskegee after that weekend, realizing I left my trusty Dora blanket. That blanket goes with me everywhere. Call me childish if you want. But to me, that was a little sign that I left a piece of my heart.

It might've been at that moment that I actually began to fall for Ford. Every two weeks or at least every month, we were making trips to see each other. We would both graduate December 2016 and make moves for our careers. He was going to be training for professional sports, while I would be getting ready to head back to KC. Surprisingly, they brought me back there to be a part of the management program. I didn't apply to work at that location, but I wasn't going to turn down a job, especially one that I was somewhat familiar with.

LIVING ON MY OWN & BILLS, CAR ISSUES & ACCIDENTS

Although I was familiar with the team and venue that I would be working with in Kansas City, I was about to take on a lot more responsibilities than I ever had. It was finally time for me to get a car. For the past couple of years, I learned how to drive by just using my ex-boyfriend and friends' cars around campus. On top of that, I couldn't use my mom's car this time around, so I had to buy my own. All of my little refund check money that I never spent went directly to buying my car. To make matters worse, a couple of weeks before I moved, I was rear ended and since the driver didn't have insurance, my mom's insurance dropped me. So, in a month I went from no bills to two, with more on the way.

My mom and I drove up to Kansas City, this time in two cars with way more than I had the last time. We searched and found an apartment. The little hopeful naïve girl in me thought my mom would help pay for the down payment or maybe a little furniture, but nope. I guess she was teaching me independence right away. I hadn't even got my first check, but all of my savings were gone. For about four years I had been saving $5 bills. It started as a New Year's Resolution. Even now, I continue this habit. But anyway, it broke my heart to break into my $5s when I moved to KC. Yes, people may call me spoiled and I never turn down money or gifts, but I absolutely HATE asking for money. I want to work for what I have and do whatever I can before having to ask someone. I finally broke down and told my sister what was going on and she helped me, both by giving me money to help and teaching me how to budget and manage my bills.

Income started coming in and with my sister's tips, I began to get the hang of adulting. I was enjoying my job at the baseball stadium, traveling to see my boyfriend every chance I got, and if I wasn't doing one of the two, I was going home to visit my family. The airport really became my best friend that year. I started getting familiar with the flight attendants. Literally, everything was in my favor during this time. As the year was coming to a close and the time came for my management program to end, a few other things were concluding as well.

JOURNAL PROMPT #6

Pros & Cons, Weighing Options

Throughout life, you will be faced with tough decisions that can alter your life in a major way. For me, I had to decide which job I would take, going back to KC or choosing a different job in Atlanta. The best way for me to weigh my options is by listing out the pros and cons. As generic as that sounds, it really is useful. Don't be afraid to ask your trusted peers & mentors for advice. Instead of completely going with one person's advice, listen to the different perspectives and take the best parts to make your decision. But most importantly, pray and ask for guidance.

Are you being faced with a tough decision? List the pros and cons, including details as well. It's also important to note how important each pro or con is to you. Rank each one 1-3, 3 being the highest, and collect the totals of each side. This way, you are factoring in the importance of each thing you listed.

_____

_____

_____

_____

_____

_____

_____

_____

_____

_____

_____

_____

PART FOUR

Heartbreak & Denver

The end of the year was coming up and my management program was ending. Depending on the need, I could stay in Kansas City or see what else was available in the company. Someone was coming in to take over my position in Kansas City, so that wasn't really the safest option. My boyfriend had made it into the league and my company had positions where he was located, so that was another option. Risky, but because our relationship was going so well, I was willing to take that step. Then a curveball came into play. There was a position in Denver that was perfect. I wasn't opposed to a new setting; however I would be moving further away from all of my loved ones.

Going into the new year, I was faced with all of these decisions and in the midst of it all, my relationship was taking a downward spiral. There had been a few lies that I caught him in. Then I saw him texting another female. The very nonchalant me calmly asked him to take me to the airport and I ignored him until I couldn't anymore. We reconciled, but things were rocky after that. I remember Ford telling me that he was "going through some things" and just needed some time. I'm huge on honesty and I asked him to just tell me if he didn't want to be in the relationship anymore. For some reason, he couldn't be honest with me right then. So, we continued to try and make it work.

As that was going on, my replacement at work started and my current job allowed me to stay over the time of my program to help train her. After carefully thinking, everything was all set for me to move to Denver. My mom and I went apartment hunting and all! The only thing I was waiting on was my offer letter. I was fine with being patient, however my lease in Kansas City was going to be up soon. I was left to figure out if I would take the risk and just move to Denver, with the hopes of being able to start there soon. Or, I could ask my cousin to stay at his place until I had more confirmation.

Eventually, my boss in Kansas City offered me the option to continue work at that account. I decided to stay with the hopes of hearing back from Denver soon. I had been staying at my cousin's house for almost a month when him, my other cousins, and our uncle came back to the city. It was now five people in a two-bedroom house, mind you I was the only girl. I knew this wouldn't work as the best living situation.

That next day was an emotional roller coaster for me. Since the Denver job was still taking forever, I decided to interview with Auburn University. I was even more excited about this job since it was closer to home.

But the moment that interview began, I knew it was over. There had been a mixup and the hiring manager was expecting me to have been there in person. The recruiter never booked a flight and it never occurred to me that the expectations were to be in person. That was a gut punch. Not even an hour after the disappointing interview, I received a call from a family member asking about sleeping arrangements for the night and plans for after that night. I was already overstaying my welcome, to my standards, but that call was like a slap in the face. I hadn't expected to still be in Kansas City and I didn't want to get an apartment because my job in KC wasn't perma- nent. I was stuck in limbo and almost running out of time.

Overwhelmed wasn't the word to describe my feelings the moment I got off the phone. I ran out of the office and to the closest bathroom. The second I stepped in the bathroom, tears poured out. I couldn't stop. It was like the world was moving at a rapid speed and I was caught in the middle, standing still. I called my sister, poured out my heart, packed up my things, and stayed in a hotel for the night. One of my coworkers, who is now family, opened up her house to me. I will never be able to repay her for that. It exposed me to a different family dynamic and essentially allowed me to continue my journey in KC.

After prayer and fasting, I arrived at work one day and it was like my decision was made for me. I had the most calming feeling. I knew I had to stay in Kansas City. I also would see hawks every single day perched in different spots on my drive to and from work. I knew it was a signal of confirmation and the fact that it was never flying, only perched, I knew that I needed to stay still. My coworker and her husband told me that I could stay with them for as long as I needed and I took them up on their offer. I now had a somewhat stable home and job, but my relationship was about to crumble.

JOURNAL PROMPT #7

Failure & Rejection

You won't always get every job you apply for and you may fail at some tasks, but don't let that stop you. You have to get back up, learn from your mistakes and the environment, and keep on going. A lot of times, what may seem like rejection may just be a pivot to get you back on the right path.

What failure or setback have you encountered recently? Analyze the situation and write down all of the outcomes, good or bad. Share what you have learned from this encounter and the outcomes.

_____

_____

_____

_____

_____

_____

_____

_____

_____

_____

_____

_____

_____

_____

INTUITION/GROWTH/TRANSFORMATION

Since I first moved to KC, I began writing in my journal and praying a lot more. With everything that had just recently happened, I was praying even more. Ford and I had a big argument that led us to stop talking. A week or two later, my best friend, Tae, came to visit me. You couldn't have told me that I was about to be completely blindsided. To my understanding, Ford was still going through some things and he couldn't talk to me, but he could still get on social media.

Two things about that: one, we hadn't seen each other since New Year's when things went left. Secondly, I noticed a female that had come up in a discussion before was now talking to him on social media. I really wanted to give him the benefit of doubt and since I believed we at least had a strong bond; he would have the decency to let me know if his feelings about me changed.

So, Tae came to visit and as usual, I'm posting all of our adventures. Nothing inappropriate, just showing that I'm enjoying myself, regardless of what may have been going on with Ford. Well, I saw that he posted something as well and I just knew that it was one of his petty posts, quoting song lyrics or something. To my surprise, he outdid himself. I opened his post to see him with the female from the messages months ago.

I went numb that moment. Tae told me that she knew I was lacking emotions because I didn't shed a tear, I just rushed her to hurry up and go out. I was really in disbelief. Did I not deserve an explanation? And to make it worse, my family and friends followed him on social media, so I was going to get questions immediately.

I numbed myself for a while and then occasionally, I would break down, wondering what happened for things to go so horribly. I really felt like I lost a best friend and there was nothing I could do. My pride was not going to let me say anything to him. The moment the post was made, his message was clear.

Needless to say, two years later and we still haven't spoken a word to each other.

I've been through all the emotions possible and I'd be lying if I said I still don't have a moment here and there. It's truly a process and yes, closure could be helpful, but I don't see a purpose at this point. I took that loss and held it close, but little did I know it might've been one of the biggest blessings in my life.

JOURNAL PROMPT #8

Getting In Tune With The Universe & Keeping Track Of Signs

Once you begin tapping into your spiritual side through prayer, meditation, and writing, you will begin to become one with the universe. Answers will start being right in front of your face and the universe will speak to you through numbers, animals, and signs. You just have to be silent and present enough to recognize them around you. Pay attention to things around you. Don't exactly go searching for things, but if you have a feeling something is meant for you, it just may be.

Keep track of those signs and research anything that you hear or see continuously. Write it all in your journal.

_____

_____

_____

_____

_____

_____

_____

_____

_____

_____

_____

_____

_____

_____

PART 5

New Beginning, New Job At OP

After a couple of months bouncing between departments at the stadium, a new opportunity fell into my lap. One of the convention centers in the district was looking for a Catering Sales Manager. While I had always been interested and passionate about events, I never actually held a position like this. The most I would do before is help out for the events at the stadium and during the off season, assist at the convention center for major events. Unfortunately, to truly understand and learn the convention life, you have to live it every day because there's always a new challenge. Nevertheless, I went to my interview at the convention center, scared as ever. Although I wasn't quite qualified, I have always had the willingness to learn in any given situation. This is when I learned that God knows your abilities, even if you don't. The interview turned into a normal conversation. Before I returned back to my current property, my boss and my interviewer had already talked. I remember my boss being mad at me that the interview went so well, because he knew that I would be leaving them soon to start at the convention center.

They rushed the process and after a couple of weeks, I was moving into my new office. I was slowly getting into the job, learning from my peers and taking on a few events at a time when my boss alerted us that she would be leaving. I had only been there for about a month and to make matters worse, she managed all of our high profile client events. With her leaving, the other sales manager and I would now have to split them.

If only you could have been inside of my brain. I went from basic, small events to these million dollar galas and events. Again, let me remind you that I never did sales or an actual management position in event planning. I knew that I had to just step up to the plate and give my all. I literally would pray every day on my way to work that God could walk before me and give me the strength to get through the day. I knew that at least one thing would go wrong during the event, but at least I could fix the issue when it arose. Because of my calm manner, I never lost my temper or even showed expressions, even when things might have been going down in flames. Sometimes, I would work 14-plus hour days and two straight weeks before having a day off. It became a norm for me. Because of my love for events, I didn't mind it. I didn't have much of a life outside of work anyway, so I fully dived into the job.

FREEDOM & EMBRACING LIFE

Although work consumed most of my time, for the first time I actually had friends in Kansas City and started to explore the city a little more. I had also moved into my new apartment. There was a new breath of fresh air after the break up. My friends and I went on random adventures just about every week, whether we were tailgating for the football games or trying out new clubs. None of us were from Kansas City, so everything was an experience.

One night when we were out, I met someone who showed me a different type of love and care that I hadn't experienced in a while. He came right on time, when I was questioning if I could even be loved. We shall name him Darius. The way we met was funny to me. My girls and I were at a bar when I saw him. I kept looking at him thinking he was familiar. Finally, I asked him where he was from and when it turned out we had never crossed paths, I just let it go. He continued the conversation and as we were leaving, he asked for my number. After a few weeks of hits and misses, we finally went on a date. We went to the movies, where I embarrassingly poured so much butter on my popcorn that it leaked onto the seat and stained my pants. Afterwards, he still wanted to see me. I'm not sure why, but I wasn't opposed. Something about our vibe was special and we started seeing each other just about every day. As special as this was, I knew a relationship wasn't for me at this time. So, I just enjoyed the time I had with him and embraced all of the love. I probably had more fun during these months than I had in a while. Now, as I go through life, I realize that when things are smooth sailing be prepared for God to shake things up a bit.

JOURNAL PROMPT #9

Creating A Routine

Once I started my new job I realized that having a routine was important. I needed some sort of structure in my life since my schedule was all over the place. Although you may not stick to your routine every day, having something to refer to is a start. Over time, you'll be following the routine without even thinking twice.

Write out a daily routine, starting from the time you wake up until the time you go to sleep. Be as detailed and time specific as possible.

_____

_____

_____

_____

_____

_____

_____

_____

_____

_____

_____

_____

_____

_____

PART 6

Spiritual Awakening

Living alone in Kansas City really strengthened my relationship with God. The trials and challenges I faced, moments of uncertainty, and having the responsibility to make life changing decisions left me no choice but to rely on God. I grew up going to a small southern black, Baptist church and I knew I wouldn't find that in Kansas City. Since my job required me to work on weekends, I started making time to watch sermons on Sundays via Youtube and taking notes in my journal. By doing that and just spending so much time with myself, I began to start noticing things happening around me. First it started with the hawks that I wrote about earlier. I would see them literally every day. It was really just a constant reminder that I was on the right path. Hawks represent messengers of the spirit world, as well as being able to see things from different perspectives. I needed those signs.

Another thing that started to happen was me seeing my birthdate everywhere. On clocks, work documents, car tags, and just about anything that involves numbers. It went from my birthday to angel numbers such as 444 or 333. My cousin told me to "pay attention to the signs of the times" and that advice put so much into perspective.

Being in Kansas City allowed me to block out so much of the everyday noise that I was normally around. When you're alone with yourself, you can pay attention to everything around you. You can literally tap into a new dimension. Your decisions become so much easier to make because you're more in tune with the world. You begin to realize that life is way bigger than just you. You have to trust God. Things will not always go how you expect or how you want, but you have to trust that it's all a process.

DECIDING TO MOVE BACK HOME, STEPPING OUT ON FAITH

One of the biggest spiritual moments to happen to me occured on my way to work at the convention center one morning. I had been feeling uneasy about a lot during this time and I couldn't exactly pinpoint what it was. I guess I was feeling homesick. I saw how much progress I was making in Kansas City and the network that I was building, but it wasn't exactly what I wanted. I knew that Atlanta was where I wanted to build my life and so many things I wanted to work on were being put on the back burner the longer I continued staying in Kansas City. On my way in to work that day, I began praying and then it led to crying. Honestly, that wasn't uncommon because I have a lot of prayer sessions in the car that lead to crying.

However, this time was different. The crying was uncontrollable, and it felt like my heart was ripping out of my chest. The closer I got to the convention center, the harder I cried. I had to pull over because I knew I couldn't walk into work with my eyes red and swollen. I pulled over, called my sister, and told her how I was feeling. I just needed her voice to comfort me. She told me that if I'm feeling this uneasy, then I already knew. After we got off the phone, something told me to look in my back seat and open up this laptop case that had been there for a few months. I opened it and there was a card that read "Just Breathe" and a Big Lots pamphlet that had "HOME" in big letters across the front. There was the confirmation that I needed. No questions left to ask.

In less than a month, I informed my boss that I would be moving back home and that I could stay as long as I could, but my decision was made. In June 2019, I packed up and moved back to Atlanta without a job. Now, I'm not stupid, so I made sure to save before moving. Plus I knew that I would be moving in with my mom for the time being. It was an adjustment from the comfortable life I had, but I've become so used to adapting and I don't mind humbling myself to prepare for the next level of my life.

MEDUSA PARTY/NEW JOB

Summer 2019 goes down in history. I was unemployed and living! It was probably my first time back in Atlanta consistently since high school. Let's just say, I made up for the lost time. I made sure to stay busy. Whether I was running errands for my family or starting to help my cousin with his businesses, I wasn't idle with my time. The moment I moved back, I went straight to applying for jobs. That is not for the weak. I will tell you right now, expect rejections. You have to believe that every rejection just means that the job was not meant for you! You cannot beat yourself up, because if you do, you'll be missing out on the perfect job that is waiting for you. Another thing I learned is to not take the first "good job" that you think is perfect. Take the time to really make your decision and don't forget to pray. Although you may be in a hurry to get a job and get that income rolling, you don't want to make the wrong choice either.

As the end of July approached, my job search narrowed down between two great opportunities. One was the catering coordinator at Morehouse College and the other was the Catering Manager at State

Farm Arena. The Morehouse-HBCU connection was a selling point for me. They basically were waiting for me to just say yes.

On the other hand, I always wanted to work in an arena, especially for an Atlanta professional sports team. But there was one thing that scared me: I would actually manage a staff. I had never directly managed a staff before. Truthfully, I like to work alone and just focus on myself. Even though the Leo leader in me comes naturally, I'm not a power hungry person. However, I knew this position would help push me to the next level. So I went for it.

And got an offer.

Eventually, the State Farm Arena position presented itself to not only offer a higher salary, but to grow even more as a professional. So I secured a dream job and around the same time, accomplished a personal milestone. During my time unemployed, I helped plan a party for my cousin and it was one of the best experiences ever. I was finally on the opposite side of events, being able to plan it from a client's point of view instead of being on the venue or caterer's side. I was also able to use my creativity and bring it to life. I was so in my element and with all of my previous experience, I knew the right questions to ask and what to look for. That event was the perfect kickstart for my new position. I knew that I was starting a new chapter of my life, but I was comfortable knowing I could thrive even in discomfort. My past proved that to me. No, I'm not perfect, but life has taught me so much over the past few years.

Now, I'm ready to utilize those lessons.

JOURNAL PROMPT #10

Goals & Intentions For The Future

Usually I end every journal setting goals and intentions for the future. Never stop growing and never stop aiming for the next goal. Because life throws so many curves your way, it's important to adjust if you need to. We have to embrace everything that happens, from heartbreak to achievements. We are not in control of everything we experience. Every little encounter builds more character, ultimately forming the person we are destined to be.

Finish this book by writing your goals and intentions for the future, may it be for this next year or the next 5 years.

_____

_____

_____

_____

_____

_____

_____

_____

_____

_____

_____

_____

_____

_____

YOU'RE GOLD.,

STAY SOLID.

DON'T LET THE WORLD MELT YOU."

"When the artist paints the canvas, the paint never sees the masterpiece in its fullness. It's impossible to do, but once the artist becomes a part of the canvas to help create the masterpiece, it can admire the beauty from its point of view, coming full circle. Step outside of your reality and try to see the world from different perspectives. Play your part in the world by being your true self, but create the masterpiece by utilizing your light and talents."

CPSIA information can be obtained
at www.ICGtesting.com
Printed in the USA
LVHW011227130421
684341LV00021B/1007

9 781649 909046